IARNRÓD É

Barraclo

Also by Simon Barraclough

Los Alamos Mon Amour (Salt, 2008)

Bonjour Tetris (Penned in the Margins, 2010)

Neptune Blue (Salt, 2011)

Sunspots (Penned in the Margins, 2015)

The Debris Field [co-author] (Sidekick Books, 2013)

Psycho Poetica [editor] (Sidekick Books, 2012)

Laboratorio [editor] (Sidekick Books, 2015)

For Phil, Laura, Breda and Lorraine

ISBN: 978-1-913642-65-5

Cover design by Aaron Kent

Edited & typeset by Aaron Kent

Broken Sleep Books (2021)

Broken Sleep Books Ltd
Rhydwen,
Talgarreg,
SA44 4HB
Wales

Contents

'Things never pass where you think,
nor along the paths you think.'
   – *Gilles Deleuze*

Iarnród Éireann

Simon Barraclough

Iarnród Éireann

The Spanish–Italian border was dismantled overnight
and the next day rusting flatbeds, snakes of freight,
metal fatigued as all fuck groaned into view, uncoiling wire,
pitching barriers, angle-grinding watchtowers and turrets
with migraine sparks, and the English–Nazi border was christened
with street parties of Rippers & Crippens & Mosleys & Haw-Haws.
My heart had long lapsed, too expensive to renew,
the biometrics broken down, but I had my mother's papers
and a code word she swaddled in lullabies now lost but not forgotten.
To Dublin, then! With McCabe the Assassin,
on one of the last helicopters out of Sigh Gone,
a DC-3 out of West Berlin, an old crate out of Silvertown,
wings and fuselage clogged by imperial sugar work,
a sticky crash-landing in the Liffey, doggy-paddling
down the Dodder till we found a wharf to gorge on Gorgonzola
with grinning green teeth and a bottle of Burgundy
from a sommelier who left no reflection
as the mirror-food floated towards us.

Fade to black with matt glasses of Vantablack® Guinness,
the most profound material known to man;
pints of vertical carbon nanotube
horizontally aligned by the end of the day;
a substance so dark it would razor off Narcissus's fizzog

and wear it to Carnivale; a liquid so dense
it sequesters a thousand millennia of shipwrecks
in a fleck of quantum foam; a gaze so unflinching
it could mine your deepest buried obscenities
and post them on the hymn board of every church in Ireland;
a drink so light-sapping your lips tingle with Hawking radiation
as you place the Kubrick monolith back onto the beermat.
And from its depths we conjured an extempore lament,
the gallows-dodging McCabe and I:

I hate it when people jump off the right bridge but land in the wrong river;
I hate it when people take money from other countries but sell their loan words;
I hate it when the power of Christ compels wrapping paper;
I hate it when you blanch at the thought of a feral hedgehog in the Languedoc;
I hate it when rapacious lyricists eulogise Yorkshire womanisers;
I hate it when people are devoted to pure, sky-fucking jouissance;
I hate it when men with wide ties don't share their sandwiches;
I hate it when people invoice me at midnight;
I hate it when your ten euro looks like a grilled rasher;
I hate it when people conflate a sausage crucifix with a breakfast get-out;
I hate it that Five Guys Named Moe on Grey Velvet *is not a giallo musical;*
I hate it when you send me your annual syntax bill;
I hate it when they say the sun's death will seal a trade deal with Proxima Centauri.
I hate it when the receipt number for ten Guinness is 13.

Deeper, then, sans McCabe, into the verdant vulvaland,
Iarnród Éireann from Dublino to Luimneach,
Intercity, a head full of Hell, INRI, Iron Nails Ran In,
with *Mercier and Camier* sharing my table,

all elbows and shanks, playing footsie with the sleepers,

buggering any gap with the bitching gab,

shuffling trips to the buffet car for miniatures

and sticking up the trolley for plasticated Jamesons.

What are trains but wormholes through weather?

What's a drinks trolley but a clattering CAT-scan

of your liver's livid inventory?

What are *Taytos* but body bags for tuber leprosy?

I tried to read but trainshake breeds flies from the alphabet,

juddering runes using sandwiches as treadmills,

vomiting the small print of the universe we never read

but still click **Agree**. Raindrops try to board

but have such small hands they can't carry tickets.

They clamp themselves to the gritty windows,

limpet mines triggered long-distance by light.

Light sleep broken by the brakes at Limerick Junction

where I grab somebody's bag and nearly alight

with a second life, a counterfeit self.

A good time to switch points, change the tune,

find a new electron shell to bat about above my crib.

Hitting 50 I'm fusing iron at the core,

can feel my organs turning over in their sleep,

hitting snooze on cell regeneration,

shouldering into flesh duvets to snatch an hour more.

My heart is scared to go out these days

for fear of who might be on the landing, on the stairs;

peeps through net curtains to see if the coast is clear.

It should be nailed beneath floorboards, telling tales

in the splintered dark with a murdered cat for company.
Maybe if I'd had children I would be braver of necessity?
My dad thought I was 'soft.' I just wanted to climb trees
and learn the constellations and stay above trouble.

Trolley-bag-lugging over the Shannon
I think of my grandfather tipping my mother
from a currach into the chill swell
for her first swimming lesson. Apocryphal?
Perhaps, but I hear her splash, taste the weed
reaching down her green throat and plucking
the strings from the harp of her lungs,
stuffing sheets of lost music into a strongbox
bound with chains and burying them in the silt
to choke and rust. The Salmon of Knowledge
lashed past her face, flicking a thin cicatrix
with a fin of foresight but she misread the sign,
took it for a grinning muddy pike and in the labour
of unwisdom dropped me into the world
on the old maternal Yoni yo-yo.
Bouncing the baggage into the Strand Hotel
I'm bumped up to 'the executive floor' and a croissant on my pillow,
a Corby trouser press for my tongue or lingam,
a life-coach crouching on the foot of the bed.
Awaken in the boot of a car coasting bumps
on the way to Woodcock Hill Bog for a team-building day
of trust games, foraging and grave-digging.
And then I'm really awake to Limerick rain tapping its metres
on business-class windows, straining for rhymes in the dusk.

On with leaky red shoes into monochrome drizzle
that falls like Anna Magnani onto neorealist rubble.
A writer buys shoes every five years and these Doc Martens
have split from the miles, evolving gills on their bellies;
flounders, bottom-feeders, sand-hiders, muggers of crabs and hermits.
All the sodden way to the house my mum was raised in,
pigeonhole for a hundred birthday cards, an address
hid to memory that the hand knows, the pen knows,
the ink imprints with platelets and plasma.
One Christmas I forgot to write it down but kissed
the envelope and the card found its way to my aunty's house.
What does Lacan say about letters always arriving?
He's an awful eejit! Sure he doesn't know us from the sky above us, like.
What has Lacan to do with the peaty smell in the air?
My first taste of foreign soil, my second whiff
of the womb's perfume on a Möbius litmus strip
of Anglo-Irish, Irish-English, the whole clan
branded with an unbreakable lineage of freckles,
future sunburns, fading stigmata that bleed under UV,
flash mob the forearms to simulate Mediterranean tans,
that once had me scrubbing my cheeks with a pumice stone
and bleach so no teacher could ever ask me again,
'Were you sunbathing under a sieve?' Well,
welcome Limerick rain, seep through my insoles,
anoint my feet, trickle your peaty vortices into the wounds.

The gravelly drive, the pebbly portico,
refuge for umbrellas in the porch behind jewelled glass.
I squelch into view, am greeted by my uncle's voice,

an octave higher than you expect from a man
built like a Martello. My socks are dark, wet,
and drop onto the hall floor like stillborn moles.
'Holes in the shoes is it? Is that what we've come to?
Is that where we're at now? Holes in the shoes?
Have you seen this, Breda? Holes in the shoes!'
'Well, it's been very dry in London.' 'Holes in the shoes!'
Palpable disappointment in this Versailles of portraits
of my successful younger cousins with families and
high-powered jobs overseas. But they're not here.
I am. We are. Mother and sister and uncle and aunt,
herded together by my sudden wish
to see 'home' again at 50 before everything – if not already –
is too late. And I'm comfortable with my disappointments,
the shrivelling heads of past loves and lost chances
spiked around my hut in the heart of Kurtz's Congo.
Don't be surprised – there are kids from Bethnal Green
who can stare at rotting heads in plastic bins
and play the next level of Candy Crush.
The rain persists as Prosecco is popped and glitter from cards
gets into buttercream and my aunty gifts me Armani shave balm
and we make plans to meet her twin for lunch –
my other aunty who got lost in the choppy estuary,
couldn't clamber back on board, was drawn by the Shannon
out to sea. It's been after those girls forever.

Next day, rain gone, what passes for sun bungs up the river like gouache.
I gawp at an emerald green postbox as I wait on the corner for the sisters.
My sister, their sisters, a day devoted to this solar system of sisters.

This postbox is dressed for Saint Patrick's Day,

only lets Saint Paddy's Day cards slip like Baileys through its slit lips,

disgorges invoices, final demands, sympathy cards, *decrees nisi*,

turns all lettering, all typefaces, into green biro – that signature

of the delirious, the unjust, the psychotic, the visionary, the unacceptable,

the indefensible, the irresponsible, the energetic and indomitable.

Ever been stalked by a biro of purest green, for your sins?

Every nook and cranny where spores of words can drift and catch

and push their webby syntax overflows with self-supporting,

autofecundating moss. London postboxes are monarchists,

colonialists, tin soldiers, slavers, Beefeaters, diabetic sores, blushes of shame.

They follow orders. It's time to order lunch.

Squeezed into a booth for a waft of Amalfi coast on Limerick high street,

the five of us twitch menus and whiff the ever-present Shannon.

My aunty's eyes float over choices with the indifference of one

who has eaten enough over seven decades. What is it with all this food?

The buying, the prepping, the cooking, the serving, the eating,

the clearing, the washing, the crapping, the whole cavalcade

regurgitating itself a few hours later.

For the love of God can't you just let me feed on air, imbibe sunlight,

draw juice from the green of plants in the garden, let the insects spin

my dynamo as they flit past on their way to *their* next meal –

will the universe never be done with eating, will the black holes

never take off their bibs, lay down their knives and forks, their spoons,

skip a course, cut out carbs, fast, go on hunger strike?

I fell for a Slovene at first sight. She said she was a breatharian.

I took it for a joke, an aspiration, a sign that we sun lovers were soulmates

but I never saw a crumb pass the event horizon of her lips in eleven years.

no spaghettification	no spaghettification	no spaghettification
n	n	n
o	o	o
s	s	s
p	p	p
a	a	a
g	g	g
h	h	h
e	e	e
t	t	t
t	t	t
i	i	i
f	f	f
i	i	i
c	c	c
a	a	a
t	t	t
i	i	i
o	o	o
n	n	n

I've been trying to fast but after a week the cravings are too intense

and I binge on my unrequited scraps till I'm sick

and swallowed by shame and can't get dressed.

What thuggish god stuffed his rubber tubes into Adam and Eve?

I think my aunty knows me.

There's a moment of alignment,

equilibrium, as her eye balances

on the beam, like a pill of air

in a spirit level. *Don't look left*

to the past. Don't look right

to the future. Let's hold this gaze

of present time, this airlock,

this quarantine pod, switch off

the tick-tock of loss, the fall
of cells through the hourglass
that links the quick and the dead;
quick, this bubble will burst but
while we're here, tell me
one thing from your life,
push one seed into the soil
of time, one tendril whose skein
unspools to the Big Bang, tell me
what makes you you, pluck one spore
that was all yours: no parents,
no sisters, no husband, no children,
no nuns, no priests, no doctors,
no saints, no Gardaí, no pets,
no errands to run, nobody's needs
to shunt yours into the ditch.
'So now –'

So begins Heaney's *Beowulf*, near as dammit,
and I'm cross-leggèd in a Yorkshire classroom,
the pose of a yogic skull and crossbones.
Dog-end of the day, a murdering cloud over dull West Nab
raining ashes of missing children on the moors.
The Canadian substitute teacher makes fresh popcorn.
As we stuff our Old World mouths with untasted delights
she horripilates us with Grendel's attack on *Heorot*,
seizing thirty souls from sleep to roast them alive at home
and gorge on thighs, buttocks, livers, hearts, lips, eyeballs.
A Standard Fireworks shed explodes on the dissolve-line of the hill

and my best friend's sister loses two fingers
packing trays of *Roman Candles* and *Mine of Serpents*
into cardboard boxes for the newsagents of Huddersfield.
Each time I prised the tight square lid off a biscuit tin,
like cracking open a casket in *The Mummy*,
I thought I might find her charred fingers in the moulded plastic slot
where the Bourbons should be. Biscuits were lifebuoys
against the dread tides of night: one more cup of tea at 9 o'clock,
a bribe to hoodwink mum and dad to stay up past the watershed
but more often than not I was sunk and lay in bed by a damp wall
trying not to notice the twisted faces in the wardrobe doors,
the grimaces of the damned in the tortoiseshell marbling
with its ghoulish reflections, tongues of Hell, and melting monsters.
Nowhere was safe. Nowhere is safe. Grendel burst
into the classroom that numb November day.
Late gasp of the year. The sunsetting of childhood.

There was an escape tunnel under the Pennines,
Pied Piper clipping the tickets, the whole trip from taxi to train
through the dragon's lair of half-remembered steam
to Holyhead and Dún Laoghaire, licence plates red as Dracula's eyes,
fabled land of black hair, pale skin, blue stares, the model of my mother
on every street, in every shop, on every passing bus,
her likeness licensed for other women to use so I could be aroused
without the guillotine of tribal taboo rattling from amniotic skies.
Before landfall, the lurch of the ferry, the pulse of ocean's engine,
a vessel like a cliff, a floating border, a sentient iron island,
Geppetto's shark, Leviathan sifting cars and coaches like krill,
families and backpackers like plankton, dissolved in gastric rust

as we wait for rescue. Tilting and tipping stomachs, pipetting poisons,
mixing tinctures, finding the balance between bile and endeavour,
baleen and spleen, adventure and emetic, spewing us onto alien shore,
scrabbling like sand crabs away from the sea, a film in reverse,
trying to shake off evolution from mechanical, sand-scraped limbs.

Sand is trying to eat the world. Tiny autonomous grinding teeth.
Drill bits, beautiful and strange under the microscope, like everything.
Howard Hughes Senior hijacked the patent from nature, invented
the rotary tri-corn rock-drill bit that harnessed the rage of every cuckold
and incel to bore oil from the ground, blood from a stone.
This is how the universe looks but, with massive Moon-manatee eyes,
fumbling fat-fingered frequencies, distended lenses of need and greed
and perpetual fear we miss it all, can't reconcile reality and vision
as we clamber over the genocidal pile of the dead to get to Heaven.
Howard Hughes Junior in his screening room, corralled by pee,
haunted by the lips outside the door, the breaths outside the door,
the words outside the door. Doorknob like a virus, crowned with spikes
teething through the soft gums of the world, born not astride a grave
but into the mouth of the next nearest person, a phantastic egg
in the womb of the throat: smooth chrome one second,
puffer fish the next, shrapnelling blades into the body politic,
the body empathetic, the body pathétique, the sobbing adagio of being.

I was the first to make every movement the adagio.
Forget your marches, your waltzes, your dynamics, your tension,
your contrast, your variety, foie gras this diet of gloom,
button a tunic over your viola torso, your cello hips.
There was a time I piped at a more perilous pitch,

marching through slush-soddened streets with scraps of carols
pinched in a wonky lyre on a dinged and battered cornet –
Adeste Fideles; Stille Nacht, heilige Nacht,
Alles schläft, einsam wacht; There is a green hill
far away, without a city wall, where our dear Lord –

Drop thy pipe, thy happy pipe.
Drop thy spear, thy piercing spear.
Drop thy sponge, thy parching sponge.
The droghte of March hath perced to the roote.

So now – I'm home. Not *home* home, but *here* home.
A home withdrawn to its hole in the skirting board of history,
afraid of dinghies, of landings, invasions, glueing traps
for its monoglot tongue, gnawing off wishbone-thin limbs,
collecting a small pile of porous bones that will be melted
by snowflakes come winter. And winter is here and winter
is when I return, in new shoes, Shoes for Life – a lifetime guarantee,
a marketing spasm, that will shoe my feet into the grave, for free,
because a sister is gone, an aunty is lost, a plot hole revealed.

Back onto the Iarnród. Spare the rod and spoil the child.
But first my feet across Beckett's bridge, razor
through the optic nerve of the Liffey. Buñuelian architecture,
an ice skate across the cow eye of Moon.
Orwell hated La Sagrada Familia but you can't be right all the time;
sometimes a mason's red-hot chip catches you in the throat.
Farewell to my familiars, Mercier and Camier, hello
to whomever's birth was the death of them – Baron Samedi

plunging the engine into Freudian tunnels of bubbling black mud,

a skeleton service, South by Southwest, rushing more

out of fear of being late for the start of the end

than from dread of the end kicking off before I'm too late.

I'm back too soon. This was all supposed to be done and dusted.

The sacred family bonds piped close with caramel and tooth enamel.

The Tooth Fairy is a monster in her world, her cave strewn

with chap-fallen Act V gags, traces of gums. We're getting on,

there are no sixth acts in Anglo-Irish lives.

And so the long day closes, the road runs out, the buffers dissolve,

the sleepers separate like spliced DNA giving up the ghost.

The station was a green screen, the carriages CAD lines

in a blank simulation with no O-D matrix. We're astonied

to be gathered again. Cousins try to recognise each other

after decades of loving neglect, flick through the Rolodex

of buried anecdotes, blushing crushes, stitches and grazes

in the A&E department of contused memory.

I break the panopticon by smashing every mirror;

they piece me back together in the fragments of their eyes.

My dad crawls out of the ground and begs me for a piggy-back.

I carry him along with this coffin, this new weighty loss,

this hod-load of absent bricks that curves the spine and dislocates

the shoulder. Pallbearers sob. I've heard this sound before.

I watch my shoes. Black shoes. Black shoes tracking

from consecrated tile to municipal tarmac to patchwork pathway

to disturbed soil. Open up the ground again. Delve into the insects' world,

Earth felt the wound. Zounds! The last thing you need is a funeral.

I fly home from Shannon. When I was small I thought the river was a runway and planes splashed down and took off from green hangars of weed.

She's gone. And Sionna has gone, leaving only her wisdom, which I fly from.

Goodbye Iarnród Éireann, goodbye Abhainn na Sionainne.

Notes and Touchstones

Dialogues II by Gilles Deleuze and Claire Parnet (2007). Translated by Hugh Tomlinson and Barbara Habberjam.

The poem is configured around two triangular trips between London, Dublin and Limerick. The first trip was planned and long overdue, the second trip following hard on its heels at the behest of an unexpected funeral.

It is a tale of red shoes and black shoes and a marketing promise of 'Shoes for Life' that has since been withdrawn.

The Spanish–Italian border is a joke of mine that poet Róisín Tierney turned into an excellent poem and book called *The Spanish–Italian Border* (Arc Publications, 2014). Here the imaginary border returns under crisis.

McCabe the Assassin is a character from Samuel Beckett's story 'Dante and the Lobster.' It's also my nickname for the poet Chris McCabe. The italicised lines on page 10 were extemporised by me and Chris in a pub in Dublin the day before my 50th birthday. The Assassin has given his permission for some of his language to be reproduced.

Leo Bloom's lunch of a Gorgonzola sandwich with Burgundy at Davy Byrne's pub (*Ulysses* by James Joyce, 1922).

Is Guinness black or red? I experience it, phenomenologically, as black but apparently it is deep red.

'Iron Nails Ran In': these nails are extracted from *Ulysses*.

Mercier and Camier by Samuel Beckett (written in 1946, published in 1970).

Taytos: legendary potato crisps.

'somewhere i have never travelled, gladly beyond' by e.e. cummings (1931).

The Salmon of Knowledge: a mythic creature that dwells in the Boyne River. I have lured it from its usual waters.

Rome, Open City (Roberto Rossellini, 1945)

Heart of Darkness by Joseph Conrad (1899)

Yoni: a Sanskrit word that has been interpreted to mean the womb and the female organs of generation.

Beowulf (700–1000 AD).

Beowulf: A New Verse Translation by Seamus Heaney (1999).

Pinocchio by Carlo Collodi (1883).

Spaghettification is the process by which (in some theories) an object would be stretched and ripped apart by gravitational forces while falling into a black hole.

The Aviator (Martin Scorsese, 2004).

Waiting for Godot by Samuel Beckett (1953).

6th Symphony by Pyotr Ilyich Tchaikovsky (1893).

George Orwell: "For the first time since I had been in Barcelona I went to have a look at the cathedral – a modern cathedral, and one of the most hideous buildings in the world." (*Homage to Catalonia,* 1938).

Songs of Innocence and Experience by William Blake (1789).

A Piece of Monologue by Samuel Beckett (1979).

The Canterbury Tales by Geoffrey Chaucer (1387–1400).

Baron Samedi: played by choreographer Geoffrey Holder in *Live and Let Die* (Guy Hamilton 1973). His final scene fuses interestingly with *North by Northwest* (Alfred Hitchcock 1959).

Endgame by Samuel Beckett (1957).

Paradise Lost by John Milton (1667).

Sionna: the river goddess of the Shannon, renowned for her beauty and cunning.

Acknowledgements

Warm thanks to Broken Sleep Books and to Chris McCabe, Isobel Dixon, Róisín Tierney, Christopher Reid, Luke Heeley and Kathryn Maris for keen eyes, ears, camaraderie and encouragement.

Lay out your unrest

Lightning Source UK Ltd.
Milton Keynes UK
UKHW011043111021
392014UK00002B/45